M

MW00760952

To Becky
From Pat

With much love,
and wishes for a
joyous 2006

# IN
# HIS
# HAND

*Patti Becklund*

*But ask the animals and they will teach you,*
*or the birds of the air, and they will tell you;*
*or speak to the earth, and it will teach you,*
*or let the fish of the sea inform you.*
*Which of all these does not know*
*that the hand of the Lord has done this?*
*In His hand is the life of every creature*
*and the breath of all mankind.*

Job 12:7-10 NIV

Cover and Jacket Design: Jeffrey Mobley Design  Tulsa, OK

HENSLEY
PUBLISHING

# Introduction

These meditations, written at the rate of about one per week, are the first of approximately three hundred, and are arranged in chronological order. At the time, my husband, Jack, and I lived in the woods overlooking Elbow Creek about six miles up the Gunflint Trail from the town of Grand Marais, Minnesota. If you refer to a map, you'll find Grand Marais about 105 miles northeast of Duluth on the north shore of Lake Superior near the Canadian border.

During those years, we lived with a houseful of cats and dogs and, because of our location at the edge of the wilderness, we regularly hosted wild animals and birds of all sizes and species, including wolves, coyotes, foxes, moose, deer, woodchucks, raccoons, pine martins, squirrels, chipmunks, ravens, seagulls, pileated woodpeckers, ducks, partridges, ermine, fishers and a host of smaller birds.

We were especially blessed at being able to make friends with several black bears, who returned to spend parts of each summer with us. Our favorite bear, a female we called Little Bit, came to us as a yearling and stayed for six years, bringing first her male cub and then, two years later, a pair of cubs.

This, then, is what God showed me during our time in the North Woods.

Patti Becklund

## Dedication

For His kids who know Him and those who have yet to meet Him…and Jack, my mate.

# Contents

# The Mediator

~☙~

*There is one God and one mediator between*
*God and men, the man Christ Jesus.*

1 Timothy 2:5 NIV

~☙~

I prepared for our sixteen-hundred mile move
with our four cats by following all the "cat rules" I
could find. Put down familiar bedding. Let them
explore their new home slowly. Reassure them with
extra love. Keep all outdoor cats inside for two weeks.

Our outdoor cat, Caesar, must have read the same
book, for he showed no interest in going outside. He
busied himself inside, stalking and sniffing into
every nook and cranny.

Two weeks later, he stood at the door and
announced he was ready to see the outside world.
With some trepidation, I opened the door, whispering,
"Go with the Lord…and be careful."

Unfamiliar birds swooped down to inspect the
new visitor. A squirrel, safe atop his lofty perch,
chattered nervously.

Our cat Einstein, Caesar's best friend, monitored
Caesar's progress from inside.

It established a pattern. Each morning, Caesar goes out for his two-hour stroll, while Einstein reports his progress, running from window to window with little meows.

This morning, busy in the kitchen, I hadn't noticed the dark clouds rolling overhead. Einstein's mournful call hustled me to the door. No sign of Caesar. I glanced up as lightning split the sky. Einstein's plaintive meowing brought my attention back. But I still saw no no sign of Caesar. Then I spotted a small black shape huddling in a corner under an overhang. It was Caesar, trusting Einstein to deliver the message so that I would come and open the door.

That seems to me just like the relationship I have with God. Jesus, monitoring my progress and problems, is the mediator who watches over and talks to the Father about me.

Thank you God. You've never failed to open the door for me.

~≈~

## ∼ Life Application ∼

1. In the Old Testament (1 Samuel 2:25) Eli talked to his sons of mediation. Read this passage. What advantage do we have that Eli did not?

_____

_____

_____

_____

_____

_____

_____

2. Hebrews 9:15 describes our mediator. After you read this passage, explain.

_____

_____

_____

_____

_____

_____

_____

∼∼∼

Look up the meaning of the word "mediator" and record it in your journal. How does Jesus fulfill that role? How have you asked Him to mediate on your behalf?

# ~ Journal ~

# Waiting For The Word

~~❦~~

But for me, I will look to the Lord and
[confident] in Him I will...wait.

Micah 7:7 AMP

~~❦~~

"Now, I'm going to teach you how to fish for Walleye Pike," Jack said as he baited my hook.

After eating my first delicious walleye dinner the night before in a restaurant, I was ready to start catching my own.

"You can troll or cast, but when you find a place you know they're laying, the best way is to lower the bait to the bottom, then bring it up a foot and wait."

"Wait?" I asked, impatient already.

"Wait. You can't just plow head-first into this. If you try to hook him when he first bites, there'll be no walleye for supper. You've got to wait."

So I held the rod, waiting. The rod wiggled. Then nothing.

"He's just nudging it; wait, he'll come back."

The the pole bent with steady pressure. "Give him a little more line," Jack urged.

"Now?" I asked.

"Not yet. Wait."

I waited what seemed like forever.

"Now?" I asked in frustration.

"Now."

I pulled up and the fight began. The fish took the bait and dove. My pole literally doubled over.

"You've got a big one," Jack said, his voice rising. "Bring him in slow and keep your rod tip up."

Calmly, he talked me through bringing the fish to the side of the boat.

"I've got him. He's a beauty. You have just caught your first walleye pike."

After a wonderful supper, I sat thinking of the lesson I'd learned that day; the need to wait.

It seems God has spent a lot of time and effort trying to teach me that one. When I'm busy rushing into things, it's hard to hear the gentle murmur of His whispered , "Wait."

Wait for the walleye; wait for the house you've always dreamed of; wait for the answer to your prayers.

I don't like waiting, but God always gives me the answer, choosing the right timing…if only I will wait.

~≈~

## ~ Life Application ~

1. Psalm 37:7 and Psalm 40:1 both suggest a solution for impatience. What instructions do they give us?

   _____

   _____

   _____

   _____

   _____

   _____

   _____

2. In Isaiah 30:18, God urges us to wait. What does He offer? Why?

   _____

   _____

   _____

   _____

   _____

   _____

   _____

   _____

~≈~

We live in a world of instant gratification. Do it now. Buy it today. Yet the Lord often asks us to wait. Have you ever waited on the Lord for an answer? Use your journal to reflect on what you learned.

# ~Journal~

# Growing Trust

~≈~

*Where no wise guidance is the people fall, but
in the multitude of counselors there is safety.*
Proverbs 11:14 AMP

~≈~

As I put down the letter from my friend, the last line rolls in my mind, "Please pray for me."

Lord, I think, that's easy now, knowing You; but I remember my first tentative prayers after becoming a Christian. The doubts and questions…*Do You really answer personal prayer?…I know what the Bible says, but do You still do that today?*

Then I think of last winter and my first ice fishing trip.

I stared at my favorite summer lake, amazed at the difference. With its shiny blanket of ice, it resembled a large meadow. Patches of snow threw off sparkles like a rhinestone dress. There in the middle was our favorite fishing spot, an island. But to get there meant I had to cross the ice.

"Come on," Jack said impatiently. "I tested the ice and it's ten inches thick. It's perfectly safe."

"I could walk and follow you," I suggested.

"Get on," he quietly replied, with his no nonsense look.

I climbed tentatively on the snowmobile and said a silent prayer. We crossed safely.

Later, as we started to cut the first hole in the ice, there was a groaning and gurgling sound (like when I forget breakfast before church). I jumped up. Squinting at the shiny ice, I saw long cracks stretching outward. My feet fairly flew to the safety of the island.

Jack stood laughing. "Honest, it's safe. The sound is actually reassuring. The lake is making ice."

Right, I thought, as I cautiously walked out on it again.

I savor those memories of yesterday. I caught two fish through that hole in the ice, ate delicious hot dogs roasted on a stick over an open fire, and started to learn to trust the ice.

That ice, Lord, is just like my early experience with prayer, venturing out afraid it would give way under me. But as the ice thickened, my trust grew. And with prayers answered, seeing You move in my life, my trust in You grew, too. Through the years, You have honored every one. Sometimes Your answers are different from my expectations, but always better.

~≈~

# ~ Life Application ~

1. Jeremiah 17:5-8 warns us to trust in God and not in other people. Why is that?

_____

_____

_____

_____

_____

_____

_____

_____

2. In Psalms 56:3-4, David explains how he conquers fear. Describe this in your own words.

_____

_____

_____

_____

_____

_____

_____

_____

~≈~

Explain in your journal how you go about trusting God.

# ~ Journal ~

_____

_____

_____

_____

_____

_____

_____

_____

_____

_____

_____

_____

_____

_____

_____

_____

_____

_____

_____

_____

_____

_____

_____

_____

# Thoughts On Thanksgiving

~≈~

*Martha, Martha…Mary has chosen what is better.*

Luke 10:42 NIV

~≈~

In the hushed dawn of Thanksgiving morning, I sit quietly. My mind pictures an army of mothers, scurrying busily around their warm kitchens preparing their feasts. I, too, should be one of them. The turkey sits in mute silence, waiting. I count the family that soon will be here, but still I wait.

In my mind's eye I see another woman, long ago, preparing a meal. She glances nervously at the doorway as the guests wander in. There is Peter in the corner, James and John talking to brother Lazarus and sister Mary. Her mind starts clicking off the number for dinner. Eighteen. No, with Lazarus and Mary, there are twenty.

Bustling around the kitchen, she thinks, *I love to have Jesus for dinner, but He always travels with such a crowd, all those apostles.* Wearily sighing, she continues preparing the meal, but angry thoughts begin to surface. *I really don't mind the work, but just once, couldn't Mary help? She always just sits there at His feet.*

Her stout little body quivers in indignation as she marches over to Jesus. Her voice trembles on the corner of rage. "Master, tell Mary to come and help me," she demands.

His gazes draws slowly up until it meets hers. His voice is gentle but softly rebuking as He answers, "Martha, Martha, don't you know Mary has chosen the better part?"

Her mouth tightens, as she wonders why He must always answer in riddles. She draws in her breath, ready to answer sharply, then looks again at Jesus. On His worn face are tired lines not apparent at his last visit. Her motherly heart melts. *Well*, she thinks, *I've got just the thing. My food will certainly perk him up.*

The scene dissolves. I'm back in my kitchen with the work still undone. Oh Martha, I know that nobody really appreciated you. But you had the gift of hospitality. How well you did. Everyone wants to be a Mary, but I never recall hearing anyone wanting to be you. Well, this morning I do, and I'm going to make the best turkey dinner I have ever made.

How Jesus must have loved you Martha. Thank you for taking such good care of Him.

~∞~

## ~ Life Application ~

1. Read Acts 28:7 and Romans 12:13. What common thread of instruction runs through each one?

   _____

   _____

   _____

   _____

   _____

   _____

   _____

   _____

2. Read 1 Peter 4:9. It gives the same instruction but with one specific warning. What is it? Who are we representing with our hospitality?

   _____

   _____

   _____

   _____

   _____

   _____

   _____

   _____

~~~

Read Hebrews 13:2. Record in your journal how you can apply the message in this verse and the previous verses to your life.

# ~ Journal ~

# Cast Out My Silly Fears

~≈~

Do not worry about what to say or how to say it. At that time, you will be given what to say.

Matthew 10:19 NIV

~≈~

I glance at the clock for the fifth time in three minutes. An hour to go; time seems to be crawling on stilted legs.

Oh, why did I ever agree to help with the readings at the church? Me, with my silly fear of speaking to groups, standing in front of the whole congregation.

I'll probably stammer, just like Moses. Yes, Moses stammered. He even told God he'd need a spokesman before he would lead the people.

How about Mary, who had the honor of anointing Jesus before He died? Here was a woman who is honored many times in the Word.

Abraham, on whom God founded a nation, was an acknowledged leader, yet twice he said of Sarah (his wife), "She is my sister." Bald-faced lies because he was afraid.

Then there was macho Peter. A tough fisherman

he sliced an ear off the servant of the high priest; but when his dreams came crashing down, he denied Jesus three times. Yet he was forgiven and carried the church upon his broad shoulders.

Then of course, my favorite, David. David of the Psalms. David who suffered from insomnia and depression. David, who not only committed adultery, but then tried to cover it up with murder.

Frail, sinful men. Yet God chose them, using their strengths and absolving their weaknesses with His love and forgiveness.

He allowed them to be shown as they really were, without "cleaning up their acts." That's how we read about them in the Bible.

I, too, am frail and fearful; but I know that I am never alone, not even when I stand to speak with stammering lips.

Thank You Lord, for casting out my fears, even the silly ones.

~≈~

## ~ Life Application ~

1. In Matthew 6:27-34, Jesus talks of worry. What does He suggest?

_____

_____

_____

_____

_____

_____

_____

2. In Luke 21:14, Jesus says we can avoid worry. How?

_____

_____

_____

_____

_____

_____

_____

~≈~

What do you fear most? How will you overcome it?

# ~ Journal ~

_____
_____
_____
_____
_____
_____
_____
_____
_____
_____
_____
_____
_____
_____
_____
_____
_____
_____
_____
_____
_____
_____
_____
_____
_____
_____
_____

# The Exercise Of Attitude

~⊰~

*If God is for us, who can be against us?*
Romans 8:31 NIV

~⊰~

He appeared with no sound, his head dwarfed by the size of his rotund body. The numbing cold had caused his feathers to puff, insulating him from the chilling wind. One large-taloned foot gradually, carefully, grasped the branch as he inched his way toward the feeding box wedged in the fork of the tree. His head slowly moved from side to side, as he scanned the white drifts to spy any hint of danger.

Hunger won out, and he stepped carefully into the box, hunkering down, pecking furiously at the corn and seeds.

Once he was sheltered in the box, his feathers flattened against his head, his brown and white outline an exquisite geometric sketch.

A rifle snap of cold echoed through the pines. His head shot up, its feathers ruffled with alarm. Perfectly still, he hovered in the silence, waiting. When he was satisfied no danger lurked, he dropped his head once again to eat.

Blue jays in the branches encircled him, raucously cawing their displeasure in finding a partridge in their feeding box. He regally ignored them; they the jesters to him, the king. Then he stepped ponderously from the box to the branch, surveying the edges of the woods. Almost faster than the eye can follow, he flew directly into the snow-covered forest, leaving only the echo of his whirring wings.

How flexible he has learned to be this winter. Feeding out of a box is foreign to a partridge.

Flexibility, an attitude to strive for; one that I should remember and practice. To become flexible means I must learn to release my will in controlling a situation. I must lean and give way.

Flexibility is an exercise in faith.

There are days when I know God is in control of my world; when a letter from a friend shares what I need to hear, or when the budget somehow equals the bills.

Then there are the days when worries accumulate, decisions are deferred, and no answers appear. That's when my stomach tightens, the headache starts. All the hills have rolled into one giant mountain, and I dwell in its shadow.

Sometimes, it's hard to hear the voice that urges me to lay all the worries at His feet in prayer. To believe He is loving and working for me and in me, even though I have no visible sign. To flex atrophied faith muscles even though it hurts.

I will try to be like the partridge today and practice flexibility. For if I have faith in Him who is for me, who can be against me?

~≈~

# ~ Life Application ~

1.   The book of Hebrews, chapter 2, describes many examples of faith in God. Describe how faith influenced Noah, Abraham and Moses.

   _____

   _____

   _____

   _____

   _____

   _____

   _____

2.   In John 3:16, what reward does God promise for those who have faith in Jesus?

   _____

   _____

   _____

   _____

   _____

   _____

   _____

~∾~

   Faith requires us to be flexible and to step out where we have never gone. Think of the times you have put yourself in the Lord's hands. How did He respond?

# ~ Journal ~

# The Gift That Counts

~~~

*She will give birth to a son, and you are to give him the name, Jesus.*

Matthew 1:21 NIV

~~~

I gaze out the frost-coated window at lazily floating snowflakes. At my feet lay colorful ribbons and piles of ripped wrapping paper. Next to me on the couch is a small pile of gifts, neatly arranged. My "take" for the Christmas season.

An hour ago, they were all mysterious presents beneath the tree. Gifts to be given, gifts to be received. I'd wondered about the large rectangular one with the silver wrappings, the red-clad square one with the beautiful bow.

So long anticipated, so quickly over.

Now a vague disappointment lingers. I'm feeling uneasy at my discontent. Did I give enough? Did I get too much? Too late to worry now. It's over in a flurry of paper and gush of "oohs" and "aahs" and "thank you's." And I find my attention wandering to the snowflakes at the window.

The snapshot of another snowy day flashes on the screen of my mind. Flakes falling in a sunshower of sequins as we drove down the trail.

Three black shapes blocked the road ahead. We stopped to watch as mother moose and her twin babies (300 pound babies at that) ambled across the road. She stretched her enormous head to nibble a slender twig at the forest's edge. The calves watched us curiously, trying to puzzle out the kind of animal our Jeep might be.

The scene was indelible, a gift that counts.

Later that same day, standing on our back deck, I'd called out, "Bertha, Bertha."

Soon a furry brown shape raced across the forest floor, climbed the spruce, leaped to the deck rail and dropped at my feet. Her race over, she waited patiently, then reached with a soft paw for my hand, knowing it would contain a peanut.

Her trust is a lasting memory, a gift that counts.

I think of the natural treasures that fill our home, unusual driftwood, knotholes of all sizes and shapes; rocks polished smooth by the restless waters of Lake Superior; the birds' nest on the mantle. All these natural treasures that delight the eyes and calm the soul; they are truly gifts that count.

Then there are the people in my life, husband, father, friends. A retired logger who shares his knowledge of the woods with me. The elderly invalid neighbor who taught me about diverse things, from birds to recipes.

These are living gifts; gifts that count.

And finally, as I look again upon the Christmas tree and the torn paper. I think of the babe in the manager who became a man and my savior, Jesus, the real gift of Christmas. As I focus on Him, the holiday becomes clear, in perspective. Slowly, the uneasy feelings disappear and peace, His peace, settles over me. Merry Christmas.

~≈~

## ~ Life Application ~

1.  Psalm 127:3 and Psalm 128:2 talk of treasures. Which treasures do you prize most dearly?

    _____

    _____

    _____

    _____

    _____

    _____

    _____

    _____

2.  In Romans 6:23, God offers us the greatest gift. What is it? How do we earn it?

    _____

    _____

    _____

    _____

    _____

    _____

    _____

    _____

~≈~

The real gift of Christmas is the birth of Jesus. What will you do this Christmas to celebrate that fact?

# ~ Journal ~

# A Matter Of Trust

~≈~

*Leaning on the entire personality of God in
absolute trust and confidence in His Power.*

Hebrews 4:2 AMP

~≈~

I sleepily stare out at the snow-laden pines. They
are dotted with patches of color, from all the birds
awaiting breakfast.

I see the tracks on the snow from Percy, our
resident partridge, who feeds on the sloppily
scattered seeds below.

Beyond are the markings of the snowshoe hare,
a nocturnal visitor snatching carrot tops. Chickadees
restlessly flit to check the empty feeder and are
jostled away by the always-impatient evening
grosbeaks. The cranberry red of the pine grosbeaks
make splashes of color on the stark limbs of the birches.

A little downy woodpecker swings on his hanging
suet ball, as his bigger cousin, a hairy woodpecker,
flies in for his turn.

I didn't know much about birds when we came
to this land, but as the seasons changed and different
flocks stopped by for a little R&R, we bought a bird
book, then a second, to identify our residents, as well
as overnight guests.

I hadn't realized, when I started to put out food in the fall, that I was training them to depend on me.

I had assumed a responsibility I hadn't understood.

My prayer time resembles the bleak landscape; no answers. It's a time to flex my spiritual muscles, to practice faith, instead of waiting to receive it.

It's a task for me to lean my entire personality on God in absolute trust; but if I can manage it, He promises great results.

I've always belonged to the school of, "I can do it myself," holding back a portion of control for myself. Yet according to the dictionary, "absolute" means no loop holes; "trust" means to expect, rely on. "Confidence" means full belief in the reliability of one looked to. Can I learn to trust, expecting God to answer? Expecting, not in anxiety, but in great excitement and anticipation, full of confidence in the belief that He will answer?

My birds rely on me to sustain them. I who am riddled with flaws. How can I dare not trust Him Who is perfect?

Rousing myself, I head for the closet to grab my coat and seed bucket to go feed our birds. As I nourish them, I am confident He will nourish me.

~≈~

## ~ Life Application ~

1. Read Psalm 22. David alternates from cries of help to affirmation of assurance and trust in God. Have you ever felt those up-and-down emotions? How did you resolve them?

_____

_____

_____

_____

_____

_____

_____

2. Look at Proverbs 3:5-6. Do you live each day that way? When you don't, what happens?

_____

_____

_____

_____

_____

_____

_____

~≈~

Think of a recent problem or crisis. Did you find a solution or did you put your trust in God? Why should you trust God with your problems?

# ~ Journal ~

# Keeping Perspective

~≈~

*In all your ways acknowledge Him, and He*
*will make your paths straight.*

Proverbs 3:6 NIV

~≈~

"Here she comes," Jack shouted.

"I can hear dogs," I responded, readying the camera where I sat perched on the crest of the seven-foot snow bank on the Greenwood road. We were waiting for the last view before the solitary forest trail claimed the woman leading in the grueling 500-mile Beargrease sled dog marathon.

"Gee, gee," she called, and her dogs responded with a graceful curve to the right, heading down a trail that led through twenty-five miles of wilderness. The sun briefly silhouetted the sixteen dogs as they snaked out of sight through the pines.

It was my first look at a sled dog race, and I was fascinated. I had taken pictures of dogs leaping in harness in their eagerness at the start of the race, and dogs curled exhausted in tight balls of fur on their beds of hay at the rest stops.

Later that night as I sat watching television, I saw

the same woman cross the finish line as the winner. Surrounded by a cheering throng and besieged by cameramen and reporters, she ignored them and pushed through the crowd to her dogs, where she hugged each one.

Jesus did a similar thing. At the height of His popularity when favorable attention was directed at Him, He pulled away to find a quiet place to talk to the Father. Later, when circumstances were reversed, He once again withdrew, this time to Gethsemane.

What do I do? How do I handle things? When my article was published and comments were favorable, did I thank the One who gave me the ideas? Or did I selfishly bask in the attention? When I received what seemed like the hundredth rejection letter, did I pray for His help? Or did I sulk and make excuses?

Unlike the lady who went first to her dogs, I am slow to fling open the door and acknowledge God's presence in the good and the bad in my life.

Thank You Father, for sled dogs, rejection slips, everything that reminds me to turn to You.

~⌇~

## ~ Life Application ~

1. In Mark 23: 6-12, Jesus talks of honor. What does He say about the scribes and Pharisees? To whom does He ascribe honor?

   _____

   _____

   _____

   _____

   _____

   _____

   _____

2. Read Psalms 35:18. Do you ever give thanks to God in public? When was the last time you did? Why?

   _____

   _____

   _____

   _____

   _____

   _____

   _____

~∞~

What do you think when you see people acknowledge God in public? Have you ever done that? How did you feel? Reflect on how you acknowledge Him and why you feel the way you do.

# ～ Journal ～

# A Spectacular Season

~~~

*To everything there is a season.*
Ecclesiastes 3:1 AMP

~~~

The snow had dusted the forest during the night, turning it into a fairyland. The sun sparkled off its surface in diamond flashes, as our snowmobile hummed along a narrow trail.

Gliding along, I could make out fresh moose tracks padding into a stand of pines; off to the right were tracks of martin and mink. The cedars wore lacy white wedding veils of snow. A free-flowing brook cut a dramatic slash through the white drifts. It was spectacular.

The last time I had been here, the leafless bushes were brown and dull. The bare ground, littered with dead leaves, had looked as though it would never give nourishment again.

The scene reminded me that there are seasons in my life, too. Sometimes, I'm in the "spring" of feelings and my faith seems to grow daily. Then there is the "summer" when I'm mellow and my trust in the Lord seems endless. In the "fall," when unseen answers to problems are hidden, I tend to drop some leaves of faith. And finally, there's "winter," when I have to trust blindly, even when answers seem lifeless. I can't hurry or force them, but must rest in the knowledge that in His time, in His spring, all will quicken and bloom again.

I whisper a quick prayer, "Thank You Lord, that there are seasons in prayer, and seasons in nature and seasons in me, and all are acceptable to You."

~≈~

## ~ Life Application ~

1.  Psalm 104:19 tells us what marks the seasons. Explain.

    _____

    _____

    _____

    _____

    _____

    _____

    _____

    _____

2.  Who does Psalm 1:2-3 describe as being like a strong tree that bears fruit in season?

    _____

    _____

    _____

    _____

    _____

    _____

    _____

    _____

~≈~

Does your faith change by season? Describe your feelings and how you see God using this time in your life.

# ~ Journal ~

# No Place Like Home

~≈~

*In My Father's house there are many dwelling places.*

John 14:2 AMP

~≈~

The floor of the deck was clear of snow and drying in the weak rays of the spring sun. I sat quietly.

Cautiously she appeared, nose twitching. Abruptly, she stopped and sat upon hind feet, reddish tail pressed against her back. Again, she moved toward my slippered foot, her long nails making tapping sounds on the deck floor.

Suddenly she chattered and scurried behind the wrought iron chair. Again, she bounced over. The peanut lay next to my foot. She ignored it, more interested in the form that had fed her through autumn and winter.

In the warm sun, an old forgotten pillow halfway emerged from its snowy quilt, a perfectly round circle drilled through its center. Earlier in the year I had watched her for days as she dug her way in, filling her cheeks with stuffing until she looked more like a chipmunk than a squirrel. Then she'd scamper away, and dive into the low-slung branches like a miniature Tarzan, intent on making her winter's home somewhere in the woods.

Just like me. I remember our move from hot, muggy Florida to the north woods of Minnesota. Starting with piles, we unpacked dishes, pictures, and clothes, and gradually made our house a home. A place where all will feel welcome.

Now I have sat looking out my office window through four seasons as the light spring leaves budded on the cherry tree, hosting in its branches woodpeckers; hummingbirds, squirrels and American goldfinches. A doe and her fawn have frisked on the driveway and ambled slowly to the garden at the fringe of the forest. Each has its home.

Jesus promises a "home" He goes to prepare. It's hard to imagine the home He is preparing for me, but somehow I believe it will be full of His creatures.

~≈~

# ∼ Life Application ∼

1. First Corinthians 16:18 and Acts 2:46 describe early Christian meetings. Where did they meet and what did they do?

_____

_____

_____

_____

_____

_____

_____

_____

2. In John 14:2, Jesus says, "I am going to prepare a place for you." Where is He going?

_____

_____

_____

_____

_____

_____

_____

_____

∼∼∼

Describe what heaven means to you.

# ~ Journal ~

# Learning To Let Go

~≈~

*My thoughts are not your thoughts, neither are your ways My ways, says the Lord.*

Isaiah 55:8 AMP

~≈~

"Well," I said, pulling off my boots, "looks as though the deer have left for the winter."

Jack turned and gently put his arm around my shoulder. "I know you're disappointed," he said, "but it's just a fact of life around here that deer will migrate down the hill for winter and return in the spring."

I knew about the migration, but it was a hard thing to accept. "I just miss seeing them every day."

Later, as I trudged up the hill toward our summer garden plot, I remembered the does that had brought their fawns in the summer.

One doe had been grazing on the hillside as her fawn frisked alongside. The fawn had begun to wander away toward the woods. Mama had continued to graze. The fawn had stepped tentatively into the underbrush and disappeared.

I'd frozen, maternal alarms ringing, but the doe

had just watched calmly, ears swiveled in the direction of her vanished offspring. She'd remained motionless for a moment, then again dipped her head to feed.

Soon the fawn had bounded back into the clearing, seemingly satisfied with the adventure, and had returned to graze at her mother's side.

Letting go is so hard for me. Why not-so-hard for the doe?

Letting go of memories, either of trials or triumphs. Letting go of control. How stubborn I can be! Like a starfish, with a thousand excuses to cling to.

It isn't easy to practice the faith needed to let God lead in every situation. It's equally hard to approach problems in faith, rather than logically or emotionally. It isn't easy to let go of the past and live in the present, much less anticipate the future.

As I neared the garden plot, I reminded myself to let go. Then I looked down and saw them. Sharp, freshly-made deer tracks leading to the corn pile.

I smiled. When I finally release problems, He always seems to have the answers. Not always the answers I expect, but the right answers at the right time.

~≈~

## ∼ Life Application ∼

1.  Proverbs 3:5 tells us not to lean on our own understanding, but to do what?

    _____

    _____

    _____

    _____

    _____

    _____

    _____

2.  Psalm 55:22 and 1 Peter 5:7 reveal a secret to life without anxiety or worry. What is it?

    _____

    _____

    _____

    _____

    _____

    _____

    _____

∼☙∼

A preacher once said, "Worry is sin because it denies the wisdom of God; it says He doesn't know what He's doing. Denies the love of God; it says He doesn't care. Denies the power of God; it says He isn't able." What do you worry about? How do you go about resolving it?

# ~ Journal ~

# A Quiet Time

~≈~

*Be still and know I am God.*
Psalm 46:10 NIV

~≈~

I tug the straps of my snowshoes over my boots and carefully trudge down the hill toward the stream. My favorite boulder has long since been layered in mounds of snow. I am content to hunker down and be quiet. The creaking of the snowshoes and the crunch of the snow are now stilled, and the immense silence of the forest covered in winter white reigns.

I settle back on my heels. "Lord, I feel discouraged. It's not that things are going wrong, it's just that I don't seem to be hitting on all cylinders. I'm in a holding pattern, like this forest in winter's grip; no trees blooming, ice freezing over the water, time suspended."

Then I remember a day in early summer when I sat on my boulder watching a mother duck leading her ducklings on an early morning swim. Another morning I shared a glance with a deer who wandered down to drink. In summer, this was a busy place. Now it lies resting. But in time, it will again bubble and run. The fish will swim in its pools. Ducklings will be born along its banks. Deer will come to drink.

The rhythms of the forest are duplicated in my life, by periods of renewal and rest, I realize. When He urges me to "Be still and know I am God" He is simply giving me time to strengthen through prayer.

It is enough.

~≈~

# ～ Life Application ～

1. Think about what Jesus tells His disciples in Mark 6:31. What does it say about quiet and solitude?

_____

_____

_____

_____

_____

_____

_____

2. Read Isaiah 18:4. Have you ever been quiet and felt God's presence? Describe your feelings.

_____

_____

_____

_____

_____

_____

_____

_____

～≈～

Think back over the past week. Did you escape the rush of your job and demands of your family to spend time with God? Did you ask Him questions and make requests? Or did you simply wait for His presence to be made known? Describe your quiet time with the Lord.

# ~ Journal ~

# Remembering To See

~∾~

*He gives to the earth snow like a blanket of wool.*

Psalm 147:16 AMP

~∾~

A gust of wind-whipped snow hit the side o the car. I shivered and huddled deeper in my jacket. The early morning dawn was blustery and dark. Just the previous night I'd made my dream lis from the seed catalog, picturing rows of green plant with large red tomatoes, tall corn stalks with silke tassels. How silly, when spring was another tw months away. Two more months of winter.

*Open your eyes and see!* The thought seemed t be running through my mind. See what? I wondere

Just then the sun threw off its blanket of cloud and a shaft of light turned the flat white snow drift into a sea of sparkling diamonds. The clouds wer peeling away, revealing a brilliant blue sky. A flock seven mallards circled by. Even the stately pine lining the road looked festive in their lacy snow shaw

It had been there all the time, but my attitude ha blocked the view. The attitude I carry into a situatio influences my perception of everything.

Attitude. A powerful word. My whole day will reflect the attitude I start with, dictating my feeling in every relationship, even my health. No wonder Romans 12:2 warns us: *Don't copy the behavior of the world, but be a different person with a fresh newness, in all you do and think.*

No, the day wasn't going to magically warm with spring-like breezes. My garden plot would still have to lie buried under its snowy quilt for a while. Spring still is two months away. Yet, there is a unique beauty in winter, a special season, if I will but remember to see.

~❧~

## ～ Life Application ～

1. Ephesians 4:22-24 encourages us to put on a new attitude. Why?

   _____

   _____

   _____

   _____

   _____

   _____

   _____

2. In Matthew 13:13-16 and in Mark 4:11-14, Jesus uses God's angry commandment as a parable. What does it teach you about seeing and perceiving?

   _____

   _____

   _____

   _____

   _____

   _____

   _____

~≫~

Think back. When was the last time you opened your spiritual eyes to see God's presence in your everyday life? What did He show you?

# ~ Journal ~

# Passing The Buck

~⊱~

Go, tell His disciples and Peter.
Mark 16:7 NIV

~⊱~

I stared at the only thing holding heat in our living room, a cup of coffee cradled in my hand.

Waking up to a chilly, fifty-three degree house had been first. Rousing Jack to our predicament was second. Rushing outside to gather firewood in the nippy twenty-one below-zero air, was third.

As we waited for the electrician, our words turned as cold and biting as the dropping temperatures.

I retreated to the couch, already disgusted with the day, and sat sipping the lukewarm coffee, thinking about Adam and Eve. Adam, always full of excuses, had said, "You gave this woman to me and she gave me the fruit." Eve's answer, "The serpent tricked me. So I ate the fruit."

The original passing of the buck. Then I remembered my earlier words. "I knew there was a funny sound in the heater last night."

Defensively, Jack had answered, "Well, why didn't you say something then?"

Doesn't seem like we've learned much since the

garden. Passing the blame may ease some of the guilt momentarily, but then one becomes even more ashamed later. The sentence that always lifts my head and helps me shake off my feeling of failure is so simple: Go, tell His disciples and Peter…

A second chance, a new beginning. Peter might have been a macho fisherman but we get peeks of his sensitivity in the gospels. He carried the knowledge of his frailties deeply. God knew Peter very well to have such an individual message of encouragement to the one who failed the worst, yet felt so much.

"…and Peter."

That could read "…and Patti."

Maybe that could even read "…and (you)."

~≈~

## ∼ Life Application ∼

1. Responsibility — or the lack of it — is mentioned throughout the Bible. What example does Judah set in Genesis 43:9? Would you do the same?

_____

_____

_____

_____

_____

_____

2. Matthew 27:3-4 gives us a tragic lesson on responsibility. Can you think of any modern-day events that parallel this? Describe them.

_____

_____

_____

_____

_____

_____

∼≫∼

Think of a time in your life when you should have taken responsibility for your actions but didn't. What should you have done? How was your life affected? Would you act differently today? Explain.

# ~ Journal ~

# Overlooking The Obvious

~≈~

*Sarah said, "God has brought me laughter ,
and everyone who hears about this will laugh
with me."*

Genesis 21:6 NIV

~≈~

"Patti, come quick." Jack's voice was low and
urgent.

Grabbing my parka, I headed for the door. As
turned to walk outside, his hand slowly pulled me
back. He motioned toward the woods. Turning my
head, I looked. The biggest bull moose I'd ever seen
stood twenty yards away, placidly returning my
stare. Knee deep in snow, he dipped his massive head
and licked the tree stump that held our salt lick.

Jack whispered, "He dug it out. Four feet of snow
covered it, and he smelled it and simply dug it out."

We stood there fascinated, watching the
magnificent animal.

His coat was deep, dark brown. The shape of his
head oddly reminded me of a horse, and his light
brown ears were long, like a donkey's. He stretched
to nuzzle a pine branch about eight feet off the
ground.

"I think he has been there since we drove in. Look

at his tracks. He's been standing there quite awhile," Jack murmured.

I shook my head in disbelief. "How do you miss seeing half-a-ton of moose?"

The next morning I read a wonderful comment of Sarah's, "God has made me laugh, everyone who hears about this will laugh with me." Neat, I thought. Sarah must have had a sense of humor. But why had I never seen that verse before? How had I missed it?

Probably just like I missed seeing a moose as big as a boxcar.

How many times do I pass by the obvious and never see, because I'm busy thinking of my own problems?

Like the time two hours had passed before I realized there had been a sad look in my friend's eyes.

Sometimes I get caught up in the squirrel-cage of my own schedule, and it blinds me to everything around.

Father, help me to see friends, Bible verses and a visiting moose, but most of all — You.

~≈~

## ~ Life Application ~

1. In Matthew 13:14, Jesus quotes the prophecy of Isaiah. What does He say about seeing and perceiving?

   _____

   _____

   _____

   _____

   _____

   _____

   _____

2. Isaiah 42:20 says, "You have seen many things, but paid no attention." Who is the prophet referring to? How does this message apply to us?

   _____

   _____

   _____

   _____

   _____

   _____

   _____

~∾~

When was the last time you stopped and really looked at God's world? What did you see? How can you be more aware of what goes on around you?

# ~ Journal ~

# Encounter With A Woodpecker

~≈~

*Thou, O Lord, art a shield about me, My glory and the One who lifts my head.*

Psalm 3:3 NASB

~≈~

I lean against the garage, looking at, but not really seeing, the woods. Instead, I remember the look of Lake Superior when a single patch of ice floated in the open water. That's the way I feel today in my spirit. Vulnerable. Adrift. Lonely.

I step into the middle of the driveway and something goes "whoosh" over my head. Startled, I duck.

A pair of pileated woodpeckers have cleared my head by inches. The male heads off into the forest. The female clings to the side of a slim birch, not ten feet away. She moves her head in puppety motions, scanning the trees. Then, for the first time I hear her call in a series of "whucker, whucker" sounds. Her large wings, spanning thirty inches, launch her soundlessly airborne to the next tree, where she makes another series of calls.

I'm amazed that she stays close to me. The bird

book describes these woodpeckers as wary, evasive and difficult to spot without careful stalking.

The last two months, she and her mate have taken turns feeding on our large hanging hunk of suet. Again, the pileated lands on our suet. She has an almost prehistoric profile. Her spearlike beak drives deeply into the frozen suet. Then, satisfied, she flies into the forest.

I shake my head in wonder at the encounter. Dark clouds scud across the sky. Wind gusts impatiently shake a covering of snow off the trees. Yet my spirit is lifted. I feel encouraged. I whisper thanks to the lifter of my head.

~≈~

## ~ Life Application ~

1. Read Job 19:13-25. Job is totally lonely and adrift until he remembers one truth. What is it?

   _____

   _____

   _____

   _____

   _____

   _____

   _____

   _____

   _____

2. In John 16:32, Jesus says He is never alone. Why not? How does this statement apply to us today?

   _____

   _____

   _____

   _____

   _____

   _____

   _____

   _____

~≈~

What is loneliness? Describe your most lonely time. What did you do?

# ~ Journal ~

# At The Weakest Moment

~∾~

*In the shadow of His hand He hid me.*
                                    Isaiah 49:2 AMP

~∾~

There is a heavy thump against the window. Our black cat, Caesar, reaches the door in one bound. He stares intently at the floor of the deck, his tail twitching.

Glancing out, I see a male grosbeak lying still. I dash for my coat, then silently slide the door open quickly closing it against Caesar's charge.

He lies still, panting with his beak open and eyes closed. I gently pick him up, cradling him in my hands. His eyes open. Then at the warmth of my hands, they slowly close again. His little body trembles.

I find myself crooning nonsense, as I did when my children were small and had hurt themselves. Then my talk turns to a whisper. "Lord, you said not even a sparrow would fall without Your knowledge. I give you this little bird and ask for his recovery."

I settle down in a weak patch of sun, loosely covering him with my scarf. Minutes pass.

He stops panting. His trembling ceases. His black

button eyes open, watching me. Gently, I lower him to the deck. He fluffs his feathers and turns his head, looking like a groggy prizefighter.

He gives me one last, brief glance, then flies to the safety of the woods.

He'll be fine.

I sit and remember life knocking me flat, leaving me to wonder if I could ever get up again. And I realize I'm a lot like that little bird. He needed comfort, the warmth of my hands, just as I need and receive God's. He holds me close until I, too, am renewed and ready to fly once again.

Funny how some of my greatest blessings have come when I'm at my weakest. Maybe that's the only time I allow Him to be strong.

~≈~

## ～ Life Application ～

1.  In 1 Corinthians 1:3-7, Paul describes how God comforts us.
    Why does God do this?

    _____

    _____

    _____

    _____

    _____

    _____

    _____

    _____

2.  Read Psalm 18:16-19. Why did God rescue David?

    _____

    _____

    _____

    _____

    _____

    _____

    _____

    _____

～❈～

Think of a time when life knocked you flat. How did God help

# ~ Journal ~

# No Doubt About It

~~≈~~

*Thomas said to Him, "Lord, we don't know where
you are going, so how can we know the way?"*
John 14:5 AMP

~~≈~~

"Isn't it a beautiful day? Look at that sun," Jack said
enthusiastically. "It's finally spring."

Dubiously, I nodded my head, thinking, *This time I'll
believe it when I see it*. Twice so far this month, I'd
thought "spring" and had been disappointed each time.

My eyes scanned our little patch of forest. All I saw
was the lingering snow heaped at the bottom of the
trees. I was eager to start our garden and see lots of green
grass, yet everywhere I looked I still saw echoes of winter
hovering all too close.

"Spring? Where?"

"Listen. Don't you see all the birds that have come
back? There's a flicker; and remember the loons on Lake
Superior?"

A few robins pecked furiously on our driveway. Our
resident partridge, Percy, sat atop a little hill, drumming
his wings to attract a mate.

"Use your imagination, your vision. Spring's all around
us. In the north, it starts with small things. That's what
makes it so important. Listen. Can you hear the creek?
We haven't heard that sound since winter froze it over."

I plopped on a chair on the back deck. Closing my eyes,

I tuned into the song of the birds. *He's right.* I thought. Instead of just blue jays and chickadees, I could pick out the song of the white throated sparrow, the twittering of the junco, even the caw of a crow.

I looked at the plastic covering the attic window and heard the thumping of flies trying to escape to find their own place in the sun. Squinting, I really looked at the birch buds, unopened, but just waiting to pop. A clump of silver willows stood in sharp relief on the side of the hills. Their bottoms were still settled in snow, but their tops reached for the sun.

I've realized I'm a lot like Thomas. He was known as a doubter, but I always thought of him as a simple man without much imagination. In John 14, Jesus said, "I go to prepare a place for you, I will come back. You know the way to the place I am going."

Thomas, dear, plain-speaking Thomas, said, "No, we don't. We haven't any idea of where you're going, so how can we know the way?"

I wonder how many times I miss what God is saying to me because I lean on my logic and close my spiritual eyes and ears.

That day, with the warmth of the sun on my face, I opened my eyes and really looked around. When I did, I saw that there were signs of spring all about me. From all the beautiful birds, to our mama deer and her yearling twins, to the patches of open ground where tenacious green clover was already struggling to establish itself. A newly-born season overflowed with life.

May I too, have a renewal…of the spirit.

## ～ Life Application ～

1. Jude 1:20-22 tells us the antidote to doubt. What are we instructed to do?

_____

_____

_____

_____

_____

_____

_____

_____

2. James 1:5-6 provides a warning to doubters. Explain.

_____

_____

_____

_____

_____

_____

_____

_____

～❧～

The disciple Thomas wasn't the only one in the Bible who had doubts. What doubts have you had in your Christian walk? How did you overcome them?

# ~ Journal ~

# Staying On Track

~⊱~

*Why do you notice the little piece of dust in your brother's eye but you don't see the big piece of wood that is in your own eye?*

Matthew 7:3 NCV

~⊱~

"Jack, come and look," I called. "We had a lot of company in our yard last night."

There were fox tracks and raccoon tracks in the sunflower seeds, and it looked like all seven deer had stopped by overnight to eat.

Walking up behind me, he slipped his arm over my shoulder and bent to peer down at the signs.

"You're becoming quite the amateur tracker."

"Maybe," I laughed, "but remember the afternoon I called and asked you to bring Dick home to check out the monster tracks?"

…It was sunset that day when I pulled into the driveway. As I was getting out of the car, I noticed fresh tracks in the snow leading toward the power lines. Strange tracks. Marks that plowed through heavy drifts. A series of prints with what appeared to be a dragged object behind them. A wolf pulling a carcass? I ran inside to phone Jack.

Soon, Dick and Jack pulled up. They got out carefully and walked next to the tracks. Dick was quiet, intently studying the line and glancing up toward the power pole

Finally, he said, "Looks like you had a visitor from the electric company. See." He pointed to the depression. "They pulled a transformer over to that pole."

My visions of a great timber wolf abruptly drained away. I was mortified. "I'm sorry. I really feel dumb."

"Hey," Jack had answered, "you're learning. At least you noticed them"…

"See how much you've learned since then," he said now, pulling me back from my memories.

"I guess what I learned is that what you see isn't always what it appears to be. Just today, I went to help a lady who was very abrupt, to say the least. Later I found out her child was quite sick."

"Yes," he agreed, "many times we make snap judgments about people, based on one quick impression. It's easy to miss the mark."

I remembered a scene from a television Easter special. The men had thrown a woman down at Jesus' feet demanding judgment. Some were even picking up rocks, ready to stone her before judgment was passed. Jesus calmly kept drawing in the sandy dirt. Looking up, He said, "Is there anyone here who has never sinned? The person without sin can throw the first stone."

Many times, I, too, form an unfair opinion because I don't know all the facts.

Lord, next time, help me remember my monster track. It's not what another person does that matters. It's how I respond.

~≈~

## ∼ Life Application ∼

1. What clear teaching does 1 Corinthians 4:4-5 give about making judgments?

_____

_____

_____

_____

_____

_____

_____

2. What common problem do both 2 Chronicles 10:8 and 16:12 point out?

_____

_____

_____

_____

_____

_____

_____

∼≈∼

What kind of person are you? Do you make hasty judgments? Do you judge others and their actions? Give a recent example and explain what the Bible says and what you should have done.

# ~ Journal ~

# The Blessing Box

~~~

*…I will open the windows of heaven for you, I will pour out more blessings than you have room for.*

Malachi 3:10 NCV

~~~

It had been a long, hard day. I went to open the garage door, thankful to be home. As usual, it stuck halfway up. Pushing with all my might, I freed the door, but my purse clicked open, scattering its contents all over the ground.

"Great! Just Great!"

The lights of Jack's truck shone as he pulled up behind me. "What's wrong?" He called.

"Nothing," I said coldly, throwing the now-dirty comb back into my purse.

"Uh, oh. Why is it when you say 'nothing' in that tone of voice it always means a great big something?" He followed me into the house.

Ramah, our Labrador, came running to greet us, her tail sending a vase on the end table crashing to the floor.

"Well, that's the kind of day it's been," I said, gesturing to the vase. "I quit. I'm going to bed and hide with a book."

"Wait a minute, I know what you need." He grabbed my hand and led me to the couch. "Wait here. I'll be right back."

As I kicked off my shoes, he set an old Kleenex box on the coffee table. It was our "blessing box."

A year earlier, I had read a magazine article about a family that wrote down each answered prayer and every special thing that happened to them.

We thought it was a good idea, so we, too, started jotting down each little blessing and stuffing them into the empty box.

I pulled out a scrap of paper and read it. "A pair of pileated woodpeckers, a gift." I remembered the day they arrived.

He pulled out a scrap and read it. "Thank You Lord, for six days of good weather, dry roads and safe travel." Another answered prayer.

I reached for another. "The deer came back again to our yard. How many people get to enjoy this blessing? Thank You."

He picked one more. "Wind is howling, forty degrees below zero, snow drifting. Thank You, Lord, for a warm safe house."

We went through the entire box, smiling and talking together.

Afterward, as I picked up our scraps of paper and stuffed them back into the box, he asked quietly, "Well, how do you feel now?"

"Peaceful, contented and very thankful," I answered. "Sometimes, I focus on only the negative things. There's much to be grateful for."

"I'm glad you got us started on this blessing box," he said. "It saved the day."

"I supplied only the box," I replied. "God provided the blessings."

# ~ Life Application ~

1. Genesis 49:25-26 tells of our earliest blessings. What are they?

_____

_____

_____

_____

_____

_____

_____

_____

2. In Malachi 3:10, God asks to be tested. What is the test? His promise?

_____

_____

_____

_____

_____

_____

_____

_____

~∾~

If you had a blessing box, what would you write down for today?

# ~Journal~

# Always Protecting

~~~

*…He will defend it, like birds flying over their nests*
Isaiah 31:5 NCV

~~~

We walked up the hill to the garden. The sun was just setting, bathing the very tops of the trees in a golden glow.

We could hear the chirps of the birds, settling down to roost for the night. The echo of a partridge's drumming hung in the still air.

"Isn't it beautiful?" Jack asked. "How lucky we are to live here in a beautiful place we both love."

At a peeping noise directly over our heads, we both glanced up.

"There!" He pointed.

A large Hairy Woodpecker was silhouetted on a poplar branch. With another loud peep, she flew in front of us, down the road. The forest grew still again, except for strange sounds coming from the tree. "Her nest, up about thirty feet," he whispered.

I squinted, "I see it, just barely, I think."

"Baby birds. Sounds like a lot of baby birds."

Just then mama landed back on the branch, seemingly disappointed we hadn't followed her. Cocking her head, she listened to the sounds drifting from a large hole in the side of the tree.

She glanced downward toward us, then with a final loud peep, she disappeared into the nest. A rising clamor of greeting, then silence.

"Our first batch of woodpecker babies." Jack chortled. "Isn't that neat?"

"Well, the first we know about anyway," I amended.

"Did you see her trying to lead us away?"

"Sure. Didn't you tell me once that a female partridge will even pretend to have a broken wing to distract you from finding her nest?"

"All creatures try to protect their young. Each has its own way. Remember yesterday, watching the aerial dog fight? Those two small birds diving and swooping to drive a bird twice their size away? Probably from their nest."

I nodded and remembered a deer, a gentle doe, rearing on her hind legs to drive away a curious yearling from her fawns. It's amazing the protectiveness God instills in adult creatures to defend their young. As humans, we are far from unique.

I thought back to when my children were young. Asthma attacks culminating in a rush to the hospital in the middle of the night. Reading, learning everything I could, protecting, sometimes too much, yet feeling reassured, knowing my Father feels the same way about me. Always watching, protecting, loving me. Even when I fall, He is always ready to forgive, forget and restore.

The feel of Jack's arm settling over my shoulder roused me from my reverie. We started down the hill to the house, content for the moment that all was right in our world.

# ~ Life Application ~

1. In Psalm 17:8, 36:8 and 61:4, David implores God to protect him. How?

_____

_____

_____

_____

_____

_____

_____

2. In Hosea 13:8, God speaks as a wronged parent. What does He threaten?

_____

_____

_____

_____

_____

_____

~∾~

In many of the Psalms, David talks of God's protection. Does God still protect His people? How does He protect you? Give an example.

# ~ Journal ~

# Giving Sanctuary

~·~·~

*…as fierce as a wild bear robbed of her cubs.*
Samuel 17:8 NIV

~·~·~

I had just lifted the little suitcase into the back of the car when I heard the noise. Our pair of nesting mallards erupted into flight off to my left. The hair on the back of my neck started to prickle. I turned slowly and there in the driveway they stood. She stared hard, not moving. Then one of her twin cubs sat up, watching me curiously.

Black bears. Mama with two cubs, and a big mama at that.

Without making a sound she charged, running in front of the cub closest to me. That such a large animal, roughly 350 pounds, could move so fast amazed me. I started waving my arms, shouting, growling and making what I hoped were threatening noises.

In struggling with the suitcase, I had left the door to the house open. *One more foot mama, and I'm gone*, I thought.

She stopped with her cubs safe behind her, watched me, then turned and left. They followed closely on her heels.

I still can't believe it. Four p.m. on a sunny May afternoon and bears in the driveway. I have seen many black bears on the North Shore, but they are usually shy, retiring animals. But this was a mother with cubs. I wish I'd had a camera to catch that black glossy coat with such a light brown face. I can't even remember the cubs, I'd been so focused on the mother.

Now I wonder what effect the bears will have on our other creatures. We've lived in our house in the woods almost two years now, and are well surrounded by animals.

The day of our arrival we were greeted by a doe and fawn grazing on the side of the hill. Now we have nine deer coming morning and evening. Then of course there's Henrietta the woodchuck, Bertha our head red squirrel who winters in the garage, and of course, Percy, resident partridge. Snowshoe hares live down the driveway. Two raccoons, last year's babies, visit nightly to snack on leftover sunflower seeds from the birds. And then there are the occasional visitors such as ermine, moose, wolves, martin and fox.

We have claimed the land as a sort of sanctuary for anything that wanders through. All are welcome to stay awhile, and most do.

But bears?

I remember the warnings we have been given. "Deer. Oh well, you'll never be able to have a garden with deer around." "Woodchucks. Boy, they'll take out that wood deck of yours." "Squirrels. They ruin things and are such pests."

Nevertheless, our garden has grown beautifully, and our deck and other outdoor accessories are still intact. The animals and birds mix and mingle almost as if they, too, feel the protection of His hand over the land.

In biblical times, the word "sanctuary" was taken literally. Three cities were set aside as safe havens for anyone who accidently, without malice, killed another.

But bears?

"Okay Lord, you gave us common sense. We'll use it to make sure no food is left around. But if sanctuary is claimed, sanctuary will be given and we'll leave the rest to you."

~≈~

# ~ Life Application ~

1. Read Psalm 16:1. How does it apply to you?

_____

_____

_____

_____

_____

_____

_____

_____


2. Deuteronomy 19:1-6 describes a safe haven. Who may be protected there?

_____

_____

_____

_____

_____

_____

_____

_____

~≈~

When you're afraid, do you have a safe haven? Describe it. When have you gone there? Why?

# ~ Journal ~

# No Matter What Name

~~~

*There followed a sharp disagreement between
them, so that they separated from each other.*

Acts 15:39 AMP

~~~

Out of the corner of my eye, I see a shape emerge from the forest. Slowly, I turn my head.

Statue still, he pauses, ears pointed forward, nose twitching. His silver coat glistens in the sunlight. He steps cautiously, quietly, first one foot, then another.

My gaze follows his mate, who silently moves to his side.

He turns his head and his golden eyes meet mine. Strength and power seem to radiate from him. We all remain frozen in place; then he breaks suddenly into a loping run. His mate is close behind. They disappear from view, swallowed by the forest.

Timber wolves. Funny, I felt no fear, just gratitude that I saw them, that I shared a piece of their world, even for a moment. I don't think I'll ever forget the look he gave me — an intelligent, weighing stare.

I wonder how many misplaced fears and suspicions we hold due to rumors that have no truth in them.

Races set against races. Religions against religions. It isn't unique with our generation. In the Bible, the early believers were set against each other.

"How were you baptized? By Peter? By Apollos? Not valid unless baptized by Peter," his followers claimed.

So it goes today — Catholic, Baptist, Lutheran.

I'm partial to Christianity myself. Many days, I don't feel worthy to call myself by Christ's name; but He loves me just the same. It's not the fall that counts, just the times you pick yourself up, asking for forgiveness, willing to try again.

"Thank You for the glimpse of the wolves, Lord. Thank You for Your churches, no matter what name they go by. You love us all."

~≈~

# ~ Life Application ~

1.  In Philippians 2:14, Paul warns against arguments. Why?

    _____

    _____

    _____

    _____

    _____

    _____

    _____

    _____


2.  What were the disciples arguing about in Mark 9:33-35? How did Jesus answer them?

    _____

    _____

    _____

    _____

    _____

    _____

    _____

    _____

~∾~

Ephesians 4:26 offers advice to live by. Describe your temper, your anger, your forgiveness.

# ~ Journal ~

# Stop And Listen

~≈~

The flowers appear on the earth, the time of
singing of the birds is come.

*Song of Songs 2:12 AMP*

~≈~

"Look what I've got," Jack said, waving a tape
in his hand.

"What is it?"

"A tape on song birds. Maybe now we can find out
what bird it was we heard everywhere last summer."

I laughed, agreeing.

For three months, wherever we were, fishing on
a quiet lake, picking blueberries, walking down a
forest trail, we kept hearing the incredible tones of
a bird we could never see.

"Aha, maybe now the mystery will be solved," I said
as he started the tape. We listened to song after song,
but nothing was quite like the one we remembered.
Then, suddenly, there it was.

"Wait, back it up. What did he say that bird is?" I
asked.

"Would you believe a white-throated sparrow? A
little bird with a big voice."

Later, as the haunting notes of the sparrow played over in my mind, I remembered my morning Bible verse. John 10:27: *My sheep know my voice and I know them.*

The Bible refers to the Lord's voice many times, Isaiah 6:8, for example: *I heard the voice of the Lord.*

But what of now? There are so many times I struggle to hear and recognize His voice above all the world's echoes. If there were only a tape I could play to identify His voice, like I can the white-throated sparrow's, then how easy it would be.

Yet, in every crisis, every time of trouble, the answer always comes. Maybe not when I demand to hear it. Maybe not the way I would have planned it, but always when I need it, so the next time a problem appears, I will know His words, or equally important, His silence. Only maybe next time He will speak a little louder, because sometimes I become a little hard of hearing from the noise of the world.

~≈~

# ~ Life Application ~

1.  John 1:1-6 explains how to recognize God's truth from
    falsehood. How is it done?

    _____

    _____

    _____

    _____

    _____

    _____

    _____

    _____

2.  Read John 10:25-58. Who did Jesus say recognized His
    voice?

    _____

    _____

    _____

    _____

    _____

    _____

    _____

~≈~

Has the Lord ever spoken to you, or in some other way made
His wishes known? How did He do this? Describe how you knew
it was Him.

# ~ Journal ~

# Practicing What You Preach

~✍~

*I am not practicing what I would like to do*
*but am doing the very thing I hate.*

Romans 7:15 NASB

~✍~

Today is one of those rare, crystal clear days. The
air is so clean, unsullied with fog or blowing dust,
that it's as though you have suddenly donned glasses
which bring everything into sharp focus.

The birch trees are dressed in their light spring
green. The aspens have taken on a slightly darker
hue, reminding me of two women not wanting to
wear the same dress.

Wild flowers peek out, stalks of drooping blue
bells and white primrose are sprinkled on the side
of the hill.

A hummingbird hangs suspended in front of his
feeder, his brilliant ruby throat making him appear
as if he were wearing a scarlet necktie.

The time of re-birth is at hand, even in the lush
carpet of grass dotted with ever-present dandelions
and a lazily droning bee that is flower shopping. It is
one of those perfect days that makes winter just a
dim memory.

Is this the same yard I spent so many winter months looking at? Then, it was a constant still life in black and white, and by March I had become impatient with the seemingly never-ending winter.

At times I become impatient with myself, too. Sometimes, demanding perfection, I am unwilling to accept my faults. I keep forgetting that just because I am striving to become more Christlike, it doesn't automatically imply I'm perfect. Tempers flare, words are spoken that shouldn't have been.

It seems then, just as Paul said: "I am not practicing what I would like to do but am doing the very thing I hate."

To be human guarantees problems, and we can be sure our shortcomings will poke through again and again.

~≈~

# ~ Life Application ~

1. Romans 7 describes Paul's see-saw struggle between how he wants to live and why he can't. Why does he struggle?

   _____

   _____

   _____

   _____

   _____

   _____

2. Paul doesn't describe his sins. We all tend to hide things we do, things that we are ashamed of. Privately list your personal stumbling blocks.

   _____

   _____

   _____

   _____

   _____

   _____

~✑~

In Romans 8 Paul gives us the answer to his dilemma. He shows us with a triumphant shout, "There is therefore now no condemnation to those who are in Christ Jesus." Describe what this means to you.

# ~ Journal ~

# A Hiding Place

*Then all of Jesus' followers left him and ran away.*

Mark 14:50 NCV

Little Bit, the cub, peeks around the side of the tall birch, thinking she is invisible. I adjust the camera lens. Out pokes an ear, then a snout. She is just as curious as I. I sit motionless, hearing the wind slough in the tops of the pines.

She nibbles on a weed, then stands on her hind legs reaching for a leafy branch. Abruptly she sits, like a large, black teddy bear, scratching at the cloud of flies that swarm all over her. A lot like Pig Pen in Charlie Brown. Her fur glistens, wet and shiny in the sun. She must have been down in the creek for a cooling bath.

"Little Bit," I whisper.

For the first time, she looks directly at me. Click. I take a picture. Her paws are huge, set on stocky legs. She's all alone now; her mother and twin have been killed. She wanders back to our yard. It's all she knows.

I let my thoughts drift in the warm afternoon sun. The disciples were scattered after Jesus was arrested. I wonder where they went? Together or alone?

We know Peter followed in the fringes of the crowd, 'til he was recognized.

We know John came and stood at the foot of the cross to say good-by.

We know that Judas died.

But where, I wonder, where were the others?

How could anyone who actually listened to Jesus, walked with Him, talked with Him, how could they have left? How could Peter denounce even knowing Him? Me, by golly, not me. I wouldn't have.

Yet…haven't I? In probably a hundred different ways. Getting angry, insisting on my own way.

Yes, I'm afraid if I'd been with the disciples, I too, would have found a hiding place in Jerusalem. Would have slowly slipped back to the upper room, not even knowing why I couldn't stay away. A lot like Little Bit.

Yet, hiding in the alleys of Jerusalem, they were as visible to God as Little Bit is to me.

~≈~

## ～ Life Application ～

1.  In Joshua 1:5 and Hebrews 13:5, God makes a promise. What is it?

    _____

    _____

    _____

    _____

    _____

    _____

    _____

2.  In John 16:32, Jesus predicts what His disciples will do. What is it? Would you have done the same?

    _____

    _____

    _____

    _____

    _____

    _____

    _____

    _____

～∾～

The disciples denounced the Lord and ran away. Have you ever run away from the Lord? Where did He find you, and how?

# ~ Journal ~

# Just Walk Outside

~≈~

*Never will I leave you; never will I forsake you.*
Hebrews 13:5 NIV

~≈~

Our backyard is quiet now, early in the morning. All the birds are nesting.

Even with three bird feeders in the back, their favorite place was our twenty-foot deck railing. I would sprinkle sunflower seeds along it, and within minutes the railing would be full of chattering birds, a communal sharing.

Interspersed amid the gaudy colors of the yellow and black grosbeaks were the soft cranberry of the purple finches, and varying shades of assorted sparrows. The front yard hosted a different crowd, all the varieties of woodpeckers and the thistle-loving goldfinches. The very air around the house was always rich in songs.

Every morning at six a.m. my alarm clock of birds gathering in the trees behind the bedroom window would wake me. Then one morning, all was quiet. The birds had gone, as if in response to a silent alarm.

I find I miss them. I stand on the deck now in the morning silence and hear an occasional cheep in the distance. I know in time they will all return and bring their young with them, but the logic of the thought and my feelings are poles apart.

I feel abandoned. Fog starts to roll in. Thunder

umbles in the distance. I move over to sit on the front tep. Suddenly, there is a rustle and a wet, furry body rawls into my lap. Long black whiskers twitching, she onfidently perches on my knee. Her dark eyes look into nine. Gently, she reaches out to touch my fingers.

"Oh Bertha, where did you come from? I didn't even ring out a nut," I say, as I stroke the squirrel's back with ny fingertip.

Then I hear the sing-song chirp of a yellow canary. here, in the cherry tree behind me, a female flies to the nistle feeder.

"Uh huh," I say. "Leaving daddy to babysit awhile. I've nissed you."

Bertha jumps down at my feet. Sitting up on her hind gs she gives her call.

"Yes," I laugh, "I know you're hungry. You're always hungry."

In the distance I hear a partridge drumming.

"Here I sit, feeling sorry for myself and all you guys re right here waiting."

It is so easy to isolate ourselves behind a pane of glass, r in the quiet of our thoughts. Isolation tends to nagnify all feelings out of proportion. The next time I el lonely, I'll try to remember to grab a sweater and alk outside. It's amazing how we can find God's touch the song of a bird…or simply in the trust of a little squirrel.

~≈~

## ～ Life Application ～

1. Read Psalm 68:6. What does God do with the lonely? Do you take advantage of this?

_____

_____

_____

_____

_____

_____

_____

2. Luke 5:16 says Jesus often withdrew to lonely places. Why

_____

_____

_____

_____

_____

_____

_____

_____

～≈～

Have you ever been totally rejected? How did you handle i
Would you do it differently today? If yes, how?

# ~ Journal ~

# Finding The Time

~~~

*There is a time for everything.*
Ecclesiastes 3:1 NIV

~~~

The granite boulders rise from the middle of the creek. The water rushes past, swollen from the recent rains. A ray of sunlight lights the center of the rock, my mediation rock. I climb on top and hunker down.

Around me, the forest is alive with early morning creatures. Birds swoop, chirping their greetings. A squirrel chatters, surprised at my entrance into his world. Bees drone by, intent on their own private searches.

I look into the quiet pool at the base of the rock where water bugs skate gracefully in circles. The morning is rich in sound and promise.

A twig snaps, as loud as a rifle shot against the quiet. I turn my head and look at a big deer which has stopped for a drink. Her coat is the rich, reddish brown of summer. She freezes, watching me. Her eyes hold a liquid softness. Then, curiosity satisfied, she bounds away.

Peace covers me and words of praise filter through my thoughts. A little oasis; this is my little oasis. My eyes sweep over the birch trees lining the banks. Their leafy tops seem to stroke the sky.

I sit remembering the past week, when I was tempted by morning sun pouring through the office window and daring me to play hooky: Wander around that bend in the creek. Follow that forest trail just to see where it goes. Think about all those fish waiting to be caught for supper. Oh, if I only could hang a "Gone Fishing" sign in the window.

Another crack. The deer again, I think. Instead, a round, black shape ambles into view.

"Little Bit. Do you get up this early or haven't you been to bed yet?"

She cocks her head, furry round ears upright, listening to my voice. Then she flops down for a satisfying scratch.

We both sit companionably for a time, simply listening to the forest sounds. I feel the air soft on my face. She sometimes lifts her head to smell the wind. Then, with a parting glance, she continues on her solitary walk following the flow of the creek.

I sit for a few minutes longer, knowing that soon I'll have to change clothes and begin my drive to work.

The secret is to be able, later in the day amidst ringing phones and errands to be run, to stop and recall the gurgling of the creek. To hear the special forest sounds. To stop and tap the source of peace in the forest. To ask for calm when confusion abounds. To ask for wisdom when there only seems to be questions. To ask for His love when there seems to be only disharmony.

The wonderful part of the secret is that God answers requests. For me, my mediation rock is my prayer closet, a cornerstone, a leveling-out place.

Yes, there is a time for work, and a time to rest. Thank you Lord, for teaching me to know the difference.

~≈~

## ~ Life Application ~

1. How does the author's "mediation rock" compare with the rock of refuge in Psalm 71:3?

_____

_____

_____

_____

_____

_____

_____

_____

2. In Psalm 46:1 and Psalm 11:1, David tells us where to find refuge. Explain.

_____

_____

_____

_____

_____

_____

_____

_____

~∽~

When you feel overwhelmed by the world, where do you find refuge? Explain how you meet God there.

# ~ Journal ~

# Still Working On It

~·~·~

My child, listen to Your Father's teaching.
Proverbs 1:8 NCV

~·~·~

"Come and take a look at this," Jack called.

"Where are you?" I asked.

"Out here on the front steps."

Drying my hands, I stepped out to join him. He patted the stoop where he was sitting.

"What—"

"Shh, it's Bertha. Watch." He pointed to the eave above the house. I could barely make out our pet squirrel's black nose; then out she tumbled, pulling a miniature squirrel with her. Trying to get a footing, she slipped, then recovered.

"She's going for the garage. She's taken two babies in there, already."

Unable to pick him up, she tried herding him, until they finally disappeared inside.

"I'm going to go in and peek."

"I'll wait here," he answered. "There's one more still up there."

Walking quietly, I stood in the dim light. I could hear scurrying, and Bertha's pips. There she was on the work bench. One baby was on the peg board as she tried to push him up toward the attic. Another was exploring the inside of a snowmobile helmet. A third was crawling on a stack of firewood. All were going in different directions, like a room of pre-schoolers. There was a large clunk as a wrench fell to the floor. Bertha's calls were reaching a higher pitch. I backed out carefully.

"You wouldn't believe the racket in there. She is running in circles, trying to get them to a new nest."

Suddenly Bertha shot out of the garage, practically flying up the side of the house, then reappeared with a baby.

She had ahold of the tiny squirrel and he had wrapped all four legs around her neck. This time she disappeared quickly into the garage.

Silence. We waited. A few minutes later she came and stretched full length at our feet, panting.

Her eyes closed. She rested.

"Poor baby, being a mother is hard work." I remembered reading somewhere that the first clue about motherhood is that it starts with the word — labor.

I thought of how many times God has tried to move me to a new place, whether it be a new attitude or thought. How hard I have fought, heels dug in, resisting all the way. Yet, I have found He makes me very uncomfortable until I learn.

Other times, I tend to run in circles like Bertha's baby in the helmet. But each time, He leads me through it, no matter how much I fear the journey.

Nope, growing up, making changes and facing problems isn't easy. I'm still working on it.

~≈~

## ~ Life Application ~

1. After Moses led his people into the desert, they began to rebel. Read Exodus 16:1-4 and Exodus 17:1-6. What instructions did he receive?

   _____

   _____

   _____

   _____

   _____

   _____

   _____

2. Hebrews 11:8-11, tells of Abraham's journey to a strange land. Why did he go? What happened to him?

   _____

   _____

   _____

   _____

   _____

   _____

   _____

~✑~

Think back to a time when the peace in your life turned to chaos. What happened? What did you do? Can you praise God for it today?

# ~ Journal ~

# So Many Questions

~～~

*...Now we see as if we are looking into a dark mirror. But at a time in the future we shall see clearly...*

1 Corinthians 13:12 NCV

~～~

It's dawn. The inbetween time. The intermission between night's formal ending and day's beginning.

We sit sipping our coffee in the dim light of the living room. There, the scraping noises come again. The cats slowly filter into the room. Ears pricked forward, they stealthily move toward the glass door. As usual, our lab sleeps soundly at our feet, totally unaware of our mysterious visitor.

The noise again. A thud.

"It's on the deck," Jack whispers. "Can you see it?"

"No." I can hear the footsteps but no shape emerges in the uncertain light.

"Well, it's not the bears or the raccoons; but something is out there."

Silence. I can see the tops of the trees beginning to sway.

"Breeze has come up." We hear the first chirping of the birds.

The flying squirrels have left. A red squirrel calls from the forest. A chipmunk scurries across the deck.

"What ever it was, it's gone now," he says.

I feel frustrated. I've never liked "the-lady-or-the-tiger" endings.

"I'm going back to bed for an hour," he says, as he kisses my cheek.

I sit on the couch; my coffee grows cold. Many mysteries, many questions and sometimes, silence instead of answers.

Why do certain things happen? Why do bad things happen to good people? The "Why" questions have filtered down through all of history.

I remember reading a story about Corri Ten Boom. Her father took her on her first train trip and she wanted to help carry their suitcase. "No," he said, kneeling down to her level. "It's too heavy for you now; wait till you grow up a bit."

Sometimes I think the answers to some of my questions might also be too heavy for me to carry. I have to trust that my Father will provide the answers when the time is right, and, possibly, when I am ready. Until then, I will have faith that He is carrying the heavy part for me.

Sunlight edges into the room. Day has officially begun. The cats leave for their secret nap places. The dog wakes, standing up, politely asking in her own way to go outside. The mystery remains unsolved for now. But there will be another early dawn, and next time, the answer may come.

~≈~

## ~ Life Application ~

1. Job 37:5 talks of acts we cannot understand. Who is responsible for these?

   _____

   _____

   _____

   _____

   _____

   _____

   _____

2. Read Matthew 13:14, Luke 8:8-10, and Mark 4:10-13. These three gospels all tell the same story. What is it, and why is it so important?

   _____

   _____

   _____

   _____

   _____

   _____

   _____

~∾~

Can you think of Bible passages you have read several times before you suddenly "saw" or understood them? What were they? Describe a specific experience.

# ~ Journal ~

# An Open Mind

~❧~

God does not see the same way people see.
People look at the outside of a person, but the
Lord looks at the heart.

1 Samuel 16:7 NCV

~❧~

"Snooks, come here quick," Jack called. "I've got the answer to our mysterious, early morning visitor."

"What, who?" I asked, thinking of a baby wolf or mink, or maybe a fisher. I quietly joined him at the patio door. The porch deck light was on and there, delicately nibbling dropped sunflower seeds, was a small skunk.

"Oh no," I murmured. "Of all the animals, I never thought of a skunk."

"Well, why not? We sure have had almost everything else. It's kind of like our very own zoo, except we're inside most times looking out."

"Oh, but Jacko, even the word 'skunk' sounds yucky."

Yet even as we watched her through the window, I was surprised by her fastidiousness. She sat and groomed her paws, looking remarkably similar to our cats. Then she just laid down with her delicately shaped head between her paws. Her coat was black and shiny, with the infamous white and black stripes as straight as if they'd been drawn with a ruler. She looked as though she could have been a sister to one of our cats.

When her nap was completed, she waddled down the deck and off to the left.

"No wonder we never could see what it was or where it went," Jack whispered. "She's made a home in the woodchuck's old hole."

I remembered how we would shine the flashlight over the back yard without ever seeing anything.

"You mean she's been here all that time?"

"Probably. She knows the layout of the deck and is obviously at home on it."

Wait one minute, Lord, I thought. Granted, I'd had grave doubts about Little Bit this summer. Then I found her to be a blessing instead of a burden. But I'd drawn the line at skunks.

I'd forgotten that one should never say never to the Lord.

I remembered a woman I'd known many years ago. I had heard that she was an extremely negative, sarcastic person. I'd started praying for her in my quiet time, then started seeing her everywhere: the grocery store, the post office, the gas station. One afternoon, while I was waiting for my dental appointment, she sat down next to me. Uncertainly, I smiled. She glared. Then a casual hello opened a torrent of words. Later, stepping into the sunshine, I shook my head. "Lord, I had no idea. All You wanted from me was a open mind."

Many times in my enthusiasm, I promise Him everything, when He only desires me to be obedient, open and willing.

I thought again about the little skunk. I had heard many horror stories about skunks, and I sure wasn't going to rush out and make friends. But maybe, as with Little Bit and the "sarcastic" woman, the stories and my preconceived notions had been exaggerated.

"Okay, Lord," I sighed, "that's your skunk and this is Your land. I'm willing to go along with Your plans, at least a day at a time."

~≈~

## ~ Life Application ~

1. In Job 38, God explains His powers to Job. What are they? Do you think God is the Almighty Creator?

   _____

   _____

   _____

   _____

   _____

   _____

   _____


2. Read Daniel 2:1-28. Daniel tells the king not to rely on fortunetellers to explain secrets. Who does he recommend? Why?

   _____

   _____

   _____

   _____

   _____

   _____

   _____

~ ∾ ~

In your journal describe a question you've asked God to answer. Has He responded yet? How?

# ～Journal～

# Continuing To Grow

~∾~

*When I was a child, I talked like a child, I thought like a child, I made plans like a child. When I became a man, I stopped those childish ways.*

1 Corinthians 13:11 NCV

~∾~

The air holds a crispness now. When I inhale, there is that snap of cold at the end of my tongue.

A subtle change of the seasons is about to begin. It shows briefly in the yellow tinge of the underbrush, and now and then a birch wears a dusting of yellow leaves.

Midday still bursts with warmth; the bees drone on their never-ending quest. The tulips of spring are long gone; the roses and irises have all dropped their petals. Now the daisies take over showing off their colors.

During the day it seems summer has just begun, but at dusk a new season quietly knocks at the door.

The birds have returned with their young, almost as big as the adults.

Wide-eyed young squirrels are introduced to the sunflower feeders by their mothers.

A porch light flipped on at night reveals a pair of young raccoons, so young their eyes hold no fear just curiosity.

One rosy dawn, a young brush wolf skittishly canters down the driveway, nose to the wind. Then at a sound heard only by him, he swerves and is swallowed up in the forest.

Later that day, a fawn, her spots almost faded away through summer's passage, wanders close to a doe's side as they make for the salt lick, which is partially visible near a thick spruce. She bends down to nip at my gift of apples at the base of the evergreen, her eyes alert and wondering.

Summer is such a short season really. The flowers and leaves give evidence that it is soon ended. But what a time of growth and change!

Sometimes I wonder if I'm still growing. I can feel the changes occur, even though I often resist them.

Lord, give me the trust and faith to accept the changes You ask, so that like the young animals, I too can grow with the seasons in my life.

~◈~

## ~ Life Application ~

1. What do Ephesians 4:14-15 and 2 Peter 3:18 tell you about growth and change?

_____

_____

_____

_____

_____

_____

_____

_____

2. Now, look at Matthew 18:3-4. What does Jesus mean in this verse? How is it an area in which you need to change?

_____

_____

_____

_____

_____

_____

_____

_____

~∞~

Think about how you react to change. Do you resist or embrace it? Are you the same person you were a year ago? Five years? Ten years? Have the changes been for the better or worse? Write your thoughts down. Be honest.

# ～Journal～

# I'm Not Perfect

~・～～

*We all stumble in many ways. If anyone does
not stumble in what he says, he is a perfect man.*

James 3:2 NASB

~・～～

"**H**ere's supper," Jack called as he loaded the
hamburgers, still fragrant from the hickory smoke,
onto plates. "You should hear the racket on the deck.
Go take a look."

I opened the screen and stepped onto the porch.
Two red squirrels were trying to climb into the same
box that contained sunflower seeds. Around and
around they chased, chattering all the while.

Finally, they settled down quietly, having solved
the problem by turning their backs to each other,
each pretending to be alone in the box.

Too bad I hadn't though of that on Monday. It had
been a busy day. Finally, a woman had come in
complaining vigorously about our small town and
the attitudes she perceived in local residents.
Instantly, I'd felt angry. How dare she judge! We might
fight amongst ourselves, but at the core, I felt, we
were really like a large extended family.

Oh Lord, I thought, I really blew it that day. Then I
remembered that a couple of my favorite people had

been in the office at the time. I cringed. Here I talk about You and write about You, but my patience is about as long as a squirrel's.

"Hey, aren't you coming in for dinner?" Jack called.

"The squirrels reminded me of our visitor at work this week."

"Oh yes," he laughed, "the rude one."

"Right, but I didn't have to respond."

He put his arm around my shoulder. "Do you remember the first meditation you wrote? It was about how Christians aren't perfect, just forgiven. I think sometimes we're too hard on ourselves when we give in to our first impulse and react like everybody else. Sure, we all strive to be the best we can, but we're still learning."

We stood quietly and I realized that the squirrels had stopped their squabbling. Peace had once again settled over the deck.

"Come on, let's go eat supper," he said.

"Right, I may not be perfect, but I sure am starving."

~≈~

## ～ Life Application ～

1. In John 8:7. Jesus admonishes the crowd. What does He say about judging others?

   _____

   _____

   _____

   _____

   _____

   _____

   _____

   _____

2. In Romans 2:1-3, Paul says people who judge others are wrong. Why? How have you been guilty of this?

   _____

   _____

   _____

   _____

   _____

   _____

   _____

   _____

～≈～

Ecclesiastes 7:20 sums up sin and righteousness. Are we all guilty? Have you ever felt unjust criticism? What did you do?

# ~ Journal ~

# Sammy's Gift

~≈~

*Do not be anxious about anything, but in
everything by prayer with thanksgiving…*
                                    Philippians 4:6 NIV

~≈~

The pillow was soft, tucked just the way I like it. The
sun-dried sheets smelled of fresh breezes. As my
thoughts tumbled toward sleep, I felt a familiar thump
next to me, and heard the rumble of Samuel's purr as he
tucked himself next to my side.

All of our cats come from Florida, but Sammy's
special. The first time I saw him, he had been trapped in
a neighbor's garage for a week. He was a wild, bedraggled
little kitten, and though I tried to catch him, he got away.

The next time I spied him, I fished him out of our car's
engine during a hard-driving rain. Again, he got away.

Then early one morning on our way to a sailboat race,
we heard a thump.

"What was that?" I asked.

Jack looked up at the rearview mirror. "Oh no, a kitten
in the engine." He braked and maneuvered the car off
the road.

I jumped out. There in the road was a struggling gray
shape. Carefully, I scooped him up. "Quick, let's get him to
the vet," I urged as I scrambled back into the car.

Later, we were told he needed his leg amputated. We

looked at each other. This was a wild, stray kitten. Did we want the responsibility, financially and emotionally?

My gaze met Jack's, and I answered, "Yes," as he nodded in agreement.

After a week, we brought him home, made a bed in the bathtub and proceeded to adopt a three-legged kitten.

Now I reached down in the dark, feeling his soft fur, hearing his contented purr. "You sure became head cat in a hurry," I mused, knowing he can run faster on three legs than the other cats can on four. His beautiful amber eyes hold more love and trust than I have ever seen any creature show. Perhaps it's a by-product of his earlier trouble.

My thoughts reviewed the different crises in my life. Never one to travel the easy road, I have always seemed to learn only through hard experience. But for everything I may have lost, I've always been blessed with something more. Different perhaps, but nevertheless treasured. For this I give thanks to a restoring God.

Granted, Sammy still has only three legs, but he possesses a compassion and capacity for love that is totally unique.

I'm grateful for the gift of Sammy, just as I'm grateful for all the wonderful people and animals He has loaned me to love.

When it comes to giving, nobody can out give our Lord.

~≈~

## ~ Life Application ~

1.  First Thessalonians 5:18 and Ephesians 5:20 tell us why we should give thanks and to whom. Explain.

_____

_____

_____

_____

_____

_____

_____

2.  In 1 Timothy 4:4, we read that everything created or provided by God is good if it is accepted in the right spirit. What unusual gift has God provided you? How has it blessed you?

_____

_____

_____

_____

_____

_____

_____

~✎~

Read Romans 8:28. Do you have a personal conflict with this message? Are you always able to apply it in your life? Explain.

# ~ Journal ~

# Change In Time

~∼~

*If any man is in Christ, he is a new creature;*
*the old things passed away.*

2 Corinthians 5:17 NASB

~∼~

There's nothing shy about fall in the North Woods. The forest explodes into vivid color.

On this gorgeous blue-gold day, I breathe in the slightly musty forest scent. The air is as crisp as the bite of a tart apple. Problems seem to have been wiped away. It's hard to carry worries when confronted with such riotous beauty.

A breeze strokes the tree tops and a cascade of leaves tumble down to my feet, like colorful snowflakes.

Change is almost palpable in the air. The maples flare orange, as if trying to rival local pumpkins. I remember early spring when they first appeared, greeting the season with their own unique shades of green.

I think back to a conversation in front of me in line at the post office a few days earlier.

"Change? He'll never change. He was ornery as a baby and he's ornery now. A leopard can't change its spots, don't you know."

Change. I scoop up a leaf, its color a burnt orange.

I think of the snowshoe hares that live behind our house. Soon, they'll display a snowy white coat of fur instead of their mottled summer brown. The deer have already exchanged their summer reddish brown for more of a graying tone.

Animals and trees can change. So too, can people. God promises He can make a new me.

I look up at the trees, noticing for the first time subtle differences. A birch stands in brassy gold, but its neighbor is a light honey-yellow, and a third still holds onto some green leaves. Each tree is on its own timetable.

Individually, they changed; at their own pace, just like people.

No, not only can't I change some things about myself, but I can't change anyone else. I can hint, harp, talk. But until the other person is ready, all my nagging won't accomplish a thing. People, like trees, have their own time schedule. I'll do better by leaving them, through prayer, to the nudging of God's Holy Spirit.

~≈~

## ～ Life Application ～

1. In Jeremiah 7:5-7, the Lord offers a reward if the people will change. How should they change? Who makes it happen?

   _____

   _____

   _____

   _____

   _____

   _____

   _____

2. First Samuel 10:6 says you will be changed into a different person. How will this happen?

   _____

   _____

   _____

   _____

   _____

   _____

   _____

～≈～

If you could change yourself and your ways, what would you change? How would you do it? If you can't, do you honestly believe God can?

# ~Journal~

# Contrasts Make The Whole

~≈~

*Now you are the body of Christ, and each one*
*of you is a part of it.*

1 Corinthians 12:27 NIV

~≈~

As we reached the crest of the hill Jack said, "Will you look at that?"

"That" was a view that looked like a painting: shades of oranges, yellows and the brassy reds of the moose maples covering both sides of the road as far as you could see.

"It's magnificent." His tone was soft and reverent. "But you know what makes it really work are the deep greens of the pines. What a contrast!"

He was right. The dark shade of the green pines punctuated the roadside, making the other trees appear even more vivid.

"A lot like us," I laughed.

"Yeah, a good marriage is a blending of two different personalities, alike in some ways and complementary in others."

"Right. My total absence of a sense of direction while you're like a homing pigeon."

"Okay, and how about your sensitivity to situations and people which keeps me from barging in like a bull moose."

"It took some work to smooth all the edges, and we're still smoothing some days, huh?"

He looked over and smiled. "Contrasts, remember?"

Contrasts. Contrasts in nature, in marriage, even in churches.

So many people, each wise in their own unique way. Just as it takes two to work at making a good marriage, it also takes many to blend a cohesive church.

I thought of the story of Paul. Trapped, he escaped out of the city at night when Christians followers lowered him over the side of the wall in a basket.

What if one of the followers had thought, "Why do I have to stay behind? I bet no one will even know my name. Paul gets all the attention."

What if he and others had decided not to help. Would Paul have escaped?

I listen with pleasure to the choir in church. I watch the ushers helping people each week. I see the flowers that beautify the altar. Then there's the potluck dinners and bake sales. It doesn't just happen.

Yes, to make a church work requires the gifts each member possesses. Contrasts, that makes a whole.

"You know, I don't care if we catch a fish. The drive itself has been worth it," Jack said. Just then big fat raindrops plopped on the windshield. "Oh, oh. Did you remember the foul weather gear? I forgot."

"Sure, it's back there with the canoe paddles and some snacks."

"Organized aren't you?" He laughed. "Just another one of those contrasts."

~≈~

## ~ Life Application ~

1. In 1 Corinthians 3:8, we are told that "He that planteth and he that watereth are one." What does that mean?

_____

_____

_____

_____

_____

_____

_____

_____

2. First Corinthians 12:12-31 talks of the body of Christ. What do we learn from it?

_____

_____

_____

_____

_____

_____

_____

_____

~≈~

What are the strengths you offer? Explain how you can use them to benefit your church.

# ~ Journal ~

# Needless Worries

~~~

*God did not give us a spirit that makes us afraid. He gave us a spirit of power and love and self-control.*

2 Timothy 1:7

~~~

I sat at the picnic table on the deck, my jacket zipped up, but the sun warm on my face. I closed my eyes and listened. A tap, tap, wasn't a woodpecker, but a blue jay cracking open sunflower seeds. Grosbeaks lined the deck, squabbling with each other, as usual.

Jack came out and pulled up a chair. "What 'cha doing?"

"Oh, thinking," I murmured.

"Little Bit?"

"How did you know?"

"Well, I miss her too, you know."

I looked toward the wood seat, which was Little Bit's favorite scratching place. She would back up to it and rub her side with the most contented look in her eye. She and her friend Skinny would appear at quarter to six, like clockwork. They would nibble the dropped sunflower seeds and Little Bit would lay at our feet.

The Lord had brought me a long way since the orphaned cub first appeared. Instead of finding her a problem, we had discovered that she was a real blessing.

Months earlier I had thought, *Bears? Not Bears!* But God was saying, "Well, we'll see."

We never treated Little Bit as a pet, and she never acted like one, but she was as curious about me as I was about her. The first attempt at friendship and communication came from her.

The first time I saw her I called her Little Bit. The next time, I called it out and she took it as her name. From then on, when I called Little Bit, she came.

Jack started to chuckle. "Remember the last time, when she came alone…"

Little Bit lay at our feet as usual. She turned her head to look across the yard and saw a second bear emerging from the forest. Jack and I recognized her friend, a male bear we called Skinny. But Little Bit woofed and snorted, jumped to her feet and started running, all in one motion. She climbed the first pine tree she came to, still woofing defensively.

Skinny stood watching, and turned his head to peer into the forest to see what had scared his friend. But there was nothing.

Our former cubs had matured into sturdy yearlings, ready to face winter hibernation. We estimated Little Bit's weight at about one hundred pounds, Skinny's about one hundred twenty-five pounds.

"In her mind," Jack said, thinking aloud, "she's still a cub. She doesn't realize how big she's grown. So when Skinny came ambling out, he looked like an adult bear to her."

It had amazed us to see this young bear react in fear, trying to climb a tree, at the sight of her friend.

I don't know why it should have surprised me. As an adult, I still do the same thing. Anticipating problems that never materialize, in my mind I run for the nearest tree. And with my imagination, I'm very good at seeing "phantom" bears.

I've had to learn to dwell in the present, forgetting the past, releasing the future. God always gives me "today" answers, not tomorrow's.

"Well, enough of this lolligagging. We've got work to do. Lets get the storm windows on," Jack said, pulling me to my feet.

"Just think, by the time we take the storm windows down again in the spring, maybe Little Bit will come back for a visit."

"Maybe," he answered slowly.

Right, I thought, I'm still learning. Guess I'd better leave spring to You.

## ～ Life Application ～

1. Leviticus 26:17 describes exactly what happens with young bears and people. What is it?

   _____

   _____

   _____

   _____

   _____

   _____

   _____

   _____

2. Verse 4 of the 23rd Psalm describes deliverance from fear. What is it?

   _____

   _____

   _____

   _____

   _____

   _____

   _____

   _____

～～～

Remember a time when you were truly afraid. How did you get past it? Have you ever used your faith in God to defeat it? Explain.

# ~Journal~

# Scattered Like Driftwood

~≈~

*Because the Lord will keep you safe. He will
keep you from being trapped.*

Proverb 3:26 NCV

~≈~

A breeze had come up and ruffled the surface of
the lake. I dug the canoe paddle in deeper.

"We'll head for the point," Jack said. "Fishing has always
been good there."

"Okay," I answered, "but look at that." I was pointing
toward the shore.

"Where? Oh, you mean that pile of driftwood? We'll
stop on the way back."

We anchored off the point and I cast out. As soon as
my lure touched the surface of the water, I felt the hit.
"I've got one." I said.

"Great," he replied. "Careful to keep your rod tip up.
Now bring it along the side of the canoe to me. All right.
I've got it and it's a beauty."

Less than a hour later, having caught and released our
limit of brook trout, we slowly paddled along the shore.

The fallen leaves had made a golden carpet, on which
a partridge goose-stepped its way to the water's edge.
There, in front of the canoe, lay several pieces of
driftwood bleached white. As the canoe edged slowly
closer, I reached out to hold us. "We've got time, can I get
out and poke around?" I asked.

"Sure, but be careful."

I stepped over the side. There lay beautiful pieces of driftwood. One looked just like a turtle. As I reached over to pick it up, my rubber boots caught on the side of a log. I lost my balance and sent wood flying in all directions.

"Are you all right?"

"Sure. Nothing hurt but my pride," I answered. "These old boots are great, but I need three pairs of socks to keep them on. I did get the 'turtle,' though."

"Wind's coming up. We better go or it will be a long, slow trip back to the landing."

Later, my face protected by my jacket collar, we paddled into the wind. I thought of driftwood emotions. Old pieces of pride, anger, or even a little resentment that I thought had weathered away years ago, suddenly surface and surprise me, tripping me up in a fall more painful than the one I experienced on the beach.

We'd like our past, our memories, to be organized and orderly like a neatly stacked pile of firewood logs. But they're not. They're scattered like driftwood, and evoke random "driftwood" feelings, some of them beautiful, some ugly.

Often we linger recalling happiness in one piece of driftwood, while another sparks anger, just like old pieces of our past, with rough edges that can trip us up.

~≈~

## ～ Life Application ～

1. Read Job 29:4-6 and Psalm 77:5. Both Job and David are unhappy. Do you blame them? Do you do the same thing?

_____

_____

_____

_____

_____

_____

_____

_____

_____

2. In Isaiah 43:18, God tells us to forget about the past. Why?

_____

_____

_____

_____

_____

_____

_____

_____

_____

～～～

Read Ecclessiates 7:10. Look back on your own life. Were you "old days" better than the present? Do you follow the message in the verse? Explain.

# ~ Journal ~

# Prayer, The Perfect Gift

~~✥~~

*Pray for each other.*
James 5:16 NCV

~~✥~~

"Yo, where are you?" I heard Jack call.

"Up here, over the garage." As I answered, I reached for a box and it tipped, scattering papers everywhere.

"What are you doing, besides making a mess?" He squatted down beside me.

"I was looking for that other strand of lights, then that box tipped. I haven't seen these notes for twenty years. I read a couple of my Christmas stories to a class of first graders. Then I asked them to write me a note about what they wanted most for Christmas. I guess I expected something like 'I want a truck,' but certainly not anything like I got."

As he quickly read a note, he raised an eyebrow. He reached for another note. "This is pretty heavy stuff for a six year old."

"I know. I was surprised, too. Listen to this one, 'Would you please pray for my little sister. There is something wrong with her. Mommy said she'd never grow up like me — but we love her anyway.'"

"How about this one? 'Mommy and Daddy don't

live in the same house anymore, something about needing more space. Please pray for a bigger house, so we can all live together again.' What did you do?" he asked.

"I prayed for them, cried a little. You just don't think kids that small can have adult-size problems."

"Well, the good part is that once you gave each one over, they were in bigger, better hands."

Later that night, I sat looking at the Christmas tree, remembering my relief after mailing off our Christmas cards. Mentally, I had scratched off another line on my holiday to-do list; but the children's notes kept replaying in my mind.

Christmas cards! Why hadn't I thought of it before? I could have given prayer as a present. Like to the friend who was going in for surgery after the holidays. I could have added a line to the card, saying "your gift will be 30 days straight of prayers for you."

I tend to be a doer. When someone needs help, I want to physically do something, like make a supper or run an errand. I sometimes tend to forget the power that is released in quiet prayer.

Prayer is a gift everyone needs but might not receive. You can never outgrow it. It always fits, and it never has to be returned, except maybe in kind.

Next time I'll tuck prayer into the Christmas cards I send.

~≈~

## ∼ Life Application ∼

1. Read Romans 1:8-10, 1 Thessalonians 1:2 and Philippians 1:3-6. When Paul wrote to these early churches, he offered a common gift. What was it? Why did he tell them?

_____

_____

_____

_____

_____

_____

_____

2. In Romans 15:30, Paul asked the church to pray for him. Do you pray for your pastor? How often? What can you pray for him?

_____

_____

_____

_____

_____

_____

_____

∼≈∼

Have you prayed for others by name? How did God answer? Are you still praying for others? Describe.

# ～Journal～

# Write It Down

| Date Made | Prayer Request | Date Received |
|-----------|----------------|---------------|
| _____ | _____ | _____ |
| _____ | _____ | _____ |
| _____ | _____ | _____ |
| _____ | _____ | _____ |
| _____ | _____ | _____ |
| _____ | _____ | _____ |
| _____ | _____ | _____ |
| _____ | _____ | _____ |
| _____ | _____ | _____ |
| _____ | _____ | _____ |
| _____ | _____ | _____ |
| _____ | _____ | _____ |
| _____ | _____ | _____ |
| _____ | _____ | _____ |
| _____ | _____ | _____ |
| _____ | _____ | _____ |
| _____ | _____ | _____ |
| _____ | _____ | _____ |
| _____ | _____ | _____ |
| _____ | _____ | _____ |
| _____ | _____ | _____ |
| _____ | _____ | _____ |

# Write It Down

| Date Made | Prayer Request | Date Received |
|-----------|----------------|---------------|
| _____ | _____ | _____ |
| _____ | _____ | _____ |
| _____ | _____ | _____ |
| _____ | _____ | _____ |
| _____ | _____ | _____ |
| _____ | _____ | _____ |
| _____ | _____ | _____ |
| _____ | _____ | _____ |
| _____ | _____ | _____ |
| _____ | _____ | _____ |
| _____ | _____ | _____ |
| _____ | _____ | _____ |
| _____ | _____ | _____ |
| _____ | _____ | _____ |
| _____ | _____ | _____ |
| _____ | _____ | _____ |
| _____ | _____ | _____ |
| _____ | _____ | _____ |
| _____ | _____ | _____ |
| _____ | _____ | _____ |
| _____ | _____ | _____ |
| _____ | _____ | _____ |
| _____ | _____ | _____ |
| _____ | _____ | _____ |

# Write It Down

| Date Made | Prayer Request | Date Received |
|-----------|----------------|---------------|
| _____ | _____ | _____ |
| _____ | _____ | _____ |
| _____ | _____ | _____ |
| _____ | _____ | _____ |
| _____ | _____ | _____ |
| _____ | _____ | _____ |
| _____ | _____ | _____ |
| _____ | _____ | _____ |
| _____ | _____ | _____ |
| _____ | _____ | _____ |
| _____ | _____ | _____ |
| _____ | _____ | _____ |
| _____ | _____ | _____ |
| _____ | _____ | _____ |
| _____ | _____ | _____ |
| _____ | _____ | _____ |
| _____ | _____ | _____ |
| _____ | _____ | _____ |
| _____ | _____ | _____ |
| _____ | _____ | _____ |
| _____ | _____ | _____ |
| _____ | _____ | _____ |
| _____ | _____ | _____ |